I0161769

Tennis:
Love Ladies
League Tennis

Sally Huss

Copyright © 2015 Sally Huss/Huss Publishing
All rights reserved.
ISBN: 0692366660
ISBN: 13: 978-0692366660

What's not to love about ladies league tennis? It offers everything women like -- exercise, fresh air, sociability, food, fashion, sport, hospitality, and anyone can participate. That is one of the most beautiful aspects of ladies league play; there is room for every level of player. Leagues are set up in levels so that all will be competing at approximately the same skill level, no matter what that is.

Who started ladies tennis leagues? It is hard to say. But, who perfected it is not! ALTA -- Atlanta Lawn Tennis Association. The association was first created in 1934 to promote tennis tournaments and junior tennis in the Atlanta area, and it started its tennis leagues in 1971 with 1,000 members. Today the membership is over 80,000. Leagues, all kinds of leagues, were developed through the years, but it was the ladies leagues that became explosive. Tennis clubs and recreation centers across the country heard about what ALTA was doing and jumped in. The group of women who ran it, figured out the formats and structures and everyone has benefited from their efforts. Rules and regulations were set up, customs were established and now zillions of women leave their kids, homes, offices, or wifely duties to run off for a morning of running around a tennis court chasing a small yellow ball, and enjoying the company of other determined sportswomen.

ALTA, a division of the USTA (United States Tennis Association) gave team tennis play its boon and now the USTA has developed a whole division devoted to league tennis, helping over 825,000 participants get on the court and play, with leagues for adults, seniors, super seniors, and mixed doubles. And probably most of the players would agree with Billie Jean King, winner of 39 Grand Slam titles, who says, "Playing on a team makes tennis MORE FUN!" She ought to know. She is the creator of World Team Tennis, a professional and amateur co-ed tennis league involving top-ranked tennis players from around the world.

League structures vary. Some play only doubles matches. Some play two singles matches and three doubles. The USTA leagues tend to include singles play, however there are other leagues within a local tennis district that are based on doubles play exclusively.

The club where I play has both kinds of leagues, however I am strictly a doubles player at this stage of my life. I bow to the ladies who volunteer to play the singles matches.

I have played ladies league tennis for about twenty of my sixty-three years of playing this fine game. As I have aged, I've moved from playing the number one position on an AA team to playing the fourth or fifth position on a 4.5 team. It's really never mattered where I played on a team or what team, as long as I got the opportunity to play.

In all of that league activity and tennis competition, I've made a few observations and have come to several conclusions or insights that might help others enjoy this strange form of the game of tennis more. The focus here is on ladies league doubles play. That's where complications can occur and the fun of partnerships come into play, literally.

I invite you to read on.

THE PLAYERS

Those who participate in league play, I've found, can be broken down into several categories of players. First, there are the Highly Competitive types. These gals can be any age, but they play to win. They come on the court ready for combat. In many cases these women/girls may be Late Bloomers, folks who never got the chance to use their competitive instincts or athletic abilities as young people, discovered tennis, and found a home. Or, these women may have been good at another sport in their youth -- soccer, baseball, even diving -- then take that competitiveness onto the court. If you've come out to have a nice social game, expect to be run over by this variety of player. These gals are not interested in the niceties of the game, but rather in the end result. They take lessons, private and group, and probably eat raw meat for breakfast.

There are a couple of other types of Highly Competitive team players, beside the Late Bloomers. These are those who recruit the just-out-of-college players to play on their teams, the Recruiters, along with the College Players themselves. Those College Players may be just as competitive as those who have recruited them. They are <u>dangerous</u> (this is assuming you are not one of them.) They hit the ball hard -- REALLY HARD. They usually play in the top positions. They have a serious presence that most Club Players are not used to. Recruit them, if you can, that is if you are interested in winning.

Then there are the Oldies-But-Goodies. I fall into this category. We are players who have seen lots of competition, may have even played on the big stage (Wimbledon, U.S. Open, etc.) but now, after kids and work, return to the courts.

These players are court savvy and know where to hit the ball and can do it. They have tricks up their sleeves -- things like drop shots, topspin lobs, slices, chops, even chips -- and can adjust to the needs of the match easily. Listen to them if you have one as a partner; their knowledge is invaluable. Not only do they know where to hit the ball, they know where to be on the court at any moment. If you are playing against such a player, hit the ball to someone else. These seasoned players can do more damage with their tricks and finesse than many of the power players.

Next, there are the everyday Club Players. Now a Club Player may not necessarily play out of a private club; she may make her home courts at the local public park. She is defined as a "Club Player" not because of where she plays, but rather that she is not a "Tournament Player," one who has seen a lot of top competition. The Club Player is someone who loves the game and has played it for years, although never getting much better or worse. Club Players' abilities are far ranging; usually they do not play in the top positions on an AA team, but fill up the roster from the third or fourth positions down. Or, they may make up the full roster of a lower-level team (4.0 or 3.0.) These players make up the bulk of ladies league participants and are the heart of league play across the country.

Then there are the trickiest and most competitive of all gals -- the Public Park Players. Again, like the Club Players, these players may not play on a public park team, but may have been raised on public park courts from infancy.

This group has little respect for the formalities of tennis, like proper strokes or known strategies. They play by the seat of their pants, hit shots you would not normally use or serve underhand, even when their shoulders don't hurt. They hit drop shots, considered a no-no in doubles, have mastered the lob, and get every ball back that comes over the net. They are usually self-taught and are very creative, having not been programmed by endless teaching pros or drills. Look out for them if you play against them; they do not follow the usual formulas of play. They thrive on delivering the unexpected. Recruit them for your team, if you can.

Those are the general categories of players that I've come in contact with during my years of league play. You, me, and every woman who has played the game falls into one of these groups or is a mixture of one or two of these groups. Keep in mind -- they all love to play.

FASHION

Fashion is a big part of ladies league tennis. Most teams pick a color combination that becomes their identifying uniform -- pink and purple, lime green and black, black and white, turquoise and peach, red and blue, etc.

Some teams pick an exact outfit that everyone on the team must purchase, have clean, and wear for their matches. This is a little harder to accomplish than just a color combination. Not surprisingly, all players on a team are not built alike. Not everyone can fit nicely into something designed for Sharapova. Form-fitting attire does not necessarily suit the stocky members of a team. Also, I have noticed, that when the season begins, players are at their best and are suited up in their respective uniforms, color coordinated, etc., but by the end of the season there might just be a hint of the required color on any member of the team. Fashion goes by the wayside when it gets down to the last matches of the season.

REFRESHMENTS

After fashion, comes food. One of the nicest parts of ladies league play is the after-the-tennis social time with refreshments. This can range from a full-out luncheon to homemade brownies, fruit, and bottled water.

Women make things nice. In whatever we do, we add "nice" to it. If you take a group of men playing in a league, they might end the event with a six-pack and a bag of chips. But, we do what comes naturally -- we are hostesses -- a vase of flowers, a platter of cheese and crackers, a bowl of homemade guacamole, along with an arrangement of fresh fruit. These are the things we learned from our mothers -- how to make things nice.

When a league match is played at some clubs, the club offers the refreshments, all turned out and professional-looking. At other clubs and many public parks, the women bring potluck style contributions -- homemade chocolate chip cookies, fresh strawberries, bunches of bananas, little bowls of sumptuous dips.

In all my years of ladies league play I have never found that there is any correlation between the quality of food and refreshments offered and the team's caliber of play. Better food does not mean better players.

Now between fashion and food there is play.

THE PLAY

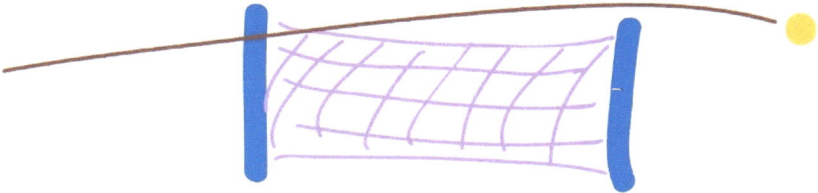

The playing of a league match has a couple of things that need to be considered before the first ball is served. Decisions have to be made. Things have to be addressed. And there are even more things to deal with once play starts. Here are a few.

BALANCING -- The Ying and the Yang of It

Playing ladies league tennis brings with it a particular decorum -- a certain sociability offset by a strong sense of competitiveness. These two may seem to be at odds with each other, but not so in league play. It is part of the structure. The host team members play the role of being hospitable, while the visitors accept to be gracious, yet each wishes to beat the heck out of the other.

Pleasantries create the desired atmosphere. This is in contrast to regular tournament play in which pleasantries are not required. Therefore, in this atmosphere of league play, a highly aggressive individual's presence is dialed down to meet the more civil and refined nature of the other participants. Balance is the result.

Balance is also the key to many aspects of league play. Both pairing and playing require balance. Partnering must come with an understanding of what the ratio of court coverage each player will undertake to handle. What is your home? And, what is mine? What am I responsible for and what are you?

This is a tricky matter; this deciding who will play where and what part of the court each will call hers. Again, niceness becomes an issue. There are two people looking at the situation with two sets of eyes -- partners. Now if you want to win, egos must be put aside and a realistic evaluation of each player's strengths and weaknesses must be considered and noted.

This is important to do each time you change partners. Every partnership creates a new formula for playing, a new balancing of strengths and adjustments for weaknesses.

Your court (half of the full tennis court) is not divided in half, as in the backhand side and the forehand side, unless you are as good and balanced as the Bryan Brothers. It is divided by how well you play and how well your partner plays. Is your partner 10%, 30% or 50% better than you? Or is she not as good and by how much? And, of course, this may not stay fixed. Your partner may be having a bad hair day that causes her to miss every backhand that comes her way. Readjust. Rebalance. The ratios may change every time you play.

The important thing to know and know very clearly is who is the stronger player and who is the weaker player on your team. Hurrah for you if you are equal! A balanced team is the hardest to beat. The greater the discrepancy between the players, a very strong player with a really weak player, the easier they are to beat. Why? Because the weaker player will be and should be played 90% of the time. No balls should go to the stronger player, outside of a serve. Not one, if you can help it, on your team or theirs. And in turn, the stronger player will find herself stretching, as she should, to take more and more balls, leaving, of course, a nice, empty court to hit to.

I suspect that most pros teaching group clinics regard all players equal in practice and do not emphasize the importance of knowing how to play in unequal partnerships.

Now if you do not know who is the weaker player on your team, play a few games and see which of you your opponents feel is weaker. They'll tell you very quickly. She'll be the one they hit all the balls to. In reality she may not be the weaker player, they just perceive her to be.

This has happened to me a couple of times where the other team had assumed that I was the stronger player because of my past tennis history, and had played my partner, the truly stronger player. They had failed to note that I had not played at Wimbledon in fifty years. Oh well, I wasn't going to point that out to them.

Again, as soon as one person is played predominantly, you or your partner (most likely it will be the weaker player,) the other player has the opportunity to take more court -- to assume more responsibility for more court. Move over, tempting your opponents to hit to the open court, which means to the stronger player.

It is kind of a cat and mouse game that the stronger member of your team gets to play -- teasing your opponents into making a sucker's move by hitting to your team's strength.

This balancing of the strong and the weak is like a dance that should go on as the ball flies back and forth across the net. It means that if you are the stronger, you slide into your partner's territory, and if you are the weaker, you relinquish some of the court, taking on only what you can comfortably handle and no more. It's a lovely idea really, if you are the weaker player and are being pounded, you have someone coming to your aid. And if you are the stronger, you are going to your partner's rescue.

These are just a few general ideas about balancing your abilities while you play.

CHOOSING SIDES -- The Intelligence of It

Here's another important consideration -- who should play which side? In practically all cases, I feel

that the stronger player should play the backhand side. That player is usually the more experienced player and has a better chance of staving off a game point when the score is 40-30 or ad-in against you, or winning a game point if it is the other way around. There are also a few exceptions to this rule. For instance, if a team is fairly balanced or if a left-hander wants to play the backhand side -- great. However, NEVER ALLOW THE WEAKER PLAYER TO MAKE CRITICAL DECISIONS! -- even if she's your best friend, or even it is you. This is especially true regarding which side to play. If the weaker player says, "But I return better from the backhand side." Nope. The stronger player can do so much more
from that side than the weaker player, provided everyone is right-handed. Besides, more critical points are played on that side of the court, and it is easier for the stronger player to keep her team in the game by bringing 40-30 and add-in points to deuce.

From the backhand side a player can poach easier at the net with her forehand into her partner's territory. And in the backcourt she can step across to take more of the shots herself. It is the stronger position traditionally and should be assigned to the stronger player.

When I play with a weaker player than myself, I play the backhand side and look to take anything I can, whether I'm at net or in the backcourt. However, if I'm lucky enough to play with one of our club's strongest players, like Lucia Romanov Stark, a former Romanian champion, I play on the right and step aside to give her every opportunity to win the point. She has a much better chance of doing that than I do. I cheer her on. This is team play. This is league play.

WARMING UP -- The Importance of It

The warm up period is a lovely opportunity to find your own rhythm for the day, and to check out your opponents. Who is the target over there? Who is the weaker player? Just as you analyzed your own partnership, you can analyze the players on the other side of the net. What are their strengths and weaknesses? This does not need to be something you jot down on your IPhone, just get a general idea of their individual abilities -- nothing too elaborate or fixed, as these may change as play begins.

First and foremost, figure out the target. Whom do you want to hit to the most often, the one who will mostly likely give you the most points? Are the players equal? Are they equal in the backcourt? Is one stronger at net? Does one hit devastating overheads? Does one move forward poorly? Just take note and pass the most useful information on to your partner, and she should do the same. So, warming up is more than tickling your own muscles, it's scouting for holes across the net.

APOLOGIZING -- The Truth of It

In tennis you never have to say you're "sorry." Nobody tries to miss a ball or double fault. This is a given. Tennis is a love story. Everyone starts with love and no one leaves the court with anything less than love. So "sorry" is not necessary.

Have you ever wondered why the word for zero in tennis is called "love"? Here it is. One of the first places tennis was ever played was in France. And, in France, as in many countries, the expression or sign for nothing or zero is an egg, a goose egg. The word for egg in French is l'oeuf, and that seems to have slid into the now more appealing word "love." There you go, now you know.

Let's look for just a moment at the essence of the saying "I'm sorry" which is so often heard on the tennis court. "I'm sorry" implies that "I could have done better." This is a little ego trick to say to others and yourself that "I'm really better than the missed shot I just hit. I'm better than that."

The truth is that you were not better at that moment. If we could truly understand that we can only do what we do at any given moment with the tensions and energies involved in that moment, including a person's experience and history of hitting tennis balls, we would never be "sorry" again. And the missed shot or double fault is merely the result, accrued from all that, in that particular moment. No "sorry" is unnecessary.

Women, being sensitive creatures that we are, do not care as much about losing a point for ourselves, but we hate to let our partners down. If you are one of these players, you might want to apologize to your partner one time before beginning the match by saying something like this: "I'll do my best. I'll try hard, but for sure I'm going to miss some balls and I might even double fault. Please forgive me. Let's play."

I played a league match against a team in which one player hit a double fault and her partner started jumping around at the net with a big grin on her face. She explained that on their club team if their teammate hits a double fault they do a "happy dance." They celebrate. They remain positive. They're smart!

I know of a teaching pro in Redondo Beach who works with kids. When they miss a ball, he calls out, "Good miss!" Every shot is a learning experience whether you are eight or eighty; so every shot in its own way is "a good shot."

You won't find a lot of "sorries" in men's matches. Get over "sorry". You're alive. You can breathe. You can run around a court. Be happy! Play happy!

Along with eliminating "being sorry," you may also wish to end rationalizing why you missed a ball. No explanations are necessary. Nobody cares. Also, there is no need to go ballistic when you win a long, laborious point or game. It can surely set you up to fall on your face a moment later. Remember, the Goldilocks Rule: not too hot and not too cold, an inner "hummm" will be just right.

We have a couple of players on our team who start out each match with a fairly cheerful attitude. As play progresses, each beats herself up with negative self-talk and obvious disappointment in her performance. By the end of the match, both of these players can barely hit a ball over the net. Besides the detrimental effect this has on their own games, they become emotional burdens to their partners, who are forever trying to bolster their spirits. It is not necessary to build yourself up with verbal self-back-patting, or knock yourself down. I've found that it's best to leave yourself alone and just play.

You may not have thought of this fact, but you have a fully conscious, working machine that you're running around in -- your body. It tries to do what you ask of it. It tries to accommodate your demands, but it is not always up to it. Be appreciative. Be kind. Be forgiving. It likes a happy camper, a happy player.

KNOWING YOUR PLACE -- The Comfort of It

One thought about being the weaker player on your team, if it is you. You need to know your place. It is not a secondary position. It's a vital position, but smaller in scope than your partner's. Everyone brings what she has to the table, to the court. You bring only what you are capable of and no more. As the weaker player of your team, you are not expected to win points. Hopefully you can keep the ball in play until the other team misses or your partner wins the point. If you win some points, great, but do not feel obligated or pressured to do so.

One of the most important things you can do is be in the right place all the time. This place moves as the play unfolds. Remember to cross over when your partner switches sides to hit a ball. Remember to close toward the center, if you are at net and the action moves from cross-court interchanges to down-the-line shots. Remember to move to your alley when the other team has a set up and is aiming at you. With these moves, you'll be doing your part, by being in the right place and giving your team the best opportunity to win the points.

HAVING EXPECTATIONS -- The Understanding of It

Expectancy is a double-edged sword. There are proponents of the idea that you must expect to win. And there are the positive thinkers who say to themselves and everyone else, "We are going to win this match!" I say that you should simply play with the intention of winning; in other words, play to win, but expect nothing. Then you are able to play freely without unnecessary pressure on yourself or your partner. Mental demands can put a burden on you that hamper your movements and decision-making as you play. Eyesight is even affected by stress. Look at all the bad calls that are made from the sheer desire to win.

On top of that, expecting to win just because you want to win sets one up for a tremendous let down if you don't win. Again, I say, play freely without expectations and see what happens. Let the results take care of themselves. Trying to control the outcome actually moves your attention away from what it should be on -- the ball -- to something that doesn't exist -- the future. Look no further ahead than the next ball and see how well you play with this attitude.

The winning and losing of a match is determined by a number of things, including intention, and everyone one has the same one. But it also has a lot to do with focused effort, energy, and a variety of athletic abilities, skill, and God-given talents. The idea is to play your best, and if you're not worried about winning, you can play your best -- relaxed and powerfully. Try it. Play full out and see what happens. That's the most fun you can have on the court.

Tennis is a game of giving rather than taking. Give freely of your efforts and let the points, games and sets come to you. Give freely of your appreciation of the efforts your opponents make. You'll feel better and play better because you feel better.

PROBLEM SOLVING -- The Necessity of It

Naturally in competitive circumstances there can arise disagreements over line calls and even the score. We are all taught and have been advised to call out the score when we are the serving team. But it doesn't happen all the time. And we are taught that calling a ball out is the responsibility of the players on that side of the net. Still disputes can crop up. My best advice regarding these issues is to give the advantage to your opponents. You'll feel better and probably play better in this more generous stance. Many of the players in ladies league are older and do not have perfect eyesight. This needs to be taken into consideration when you are questioning an opponent's call or your own. Call 'em as you see 'em and let your opponents do the same. That's easy.

Foot faults pose another challenge. Ladies league play operates on the honor system with no officials presiding over the play. If foot faults become obvious, it is probably best to bring this to the player's attention who is making this error and ask that it be corrected rather than start a full scale ruckus. Usually small infractions can be solved without much ado.

What to do about players who show up late? Fortunately there are rules that the captains must enforce on this issue. There are all kinds of excuses for this mishap -- from traffic to "my babysitter didn't show up on time" or "I got lost." My personal preference is to play a match rather than win it by default, even if the other team's member missed the curfew. It's always more fun to play.

If the idea for the day's event is to play some good tennis and have a good time then most disagreements can be settled and any emotions attached to the problem diffused successfully.

Fortunately there is a list of rules and regulations that apply to every league situation that you can imagine. However, I also imagine that the list continues to grow as the unexpected arises. As one longtime club owner, Dorothy Roth, says in regards to ladies league activity, "You think you've seen it all... but then you haven't."

STACKING -- The Nonsense of It

Stacking is the intentional maneuvering of players out of their proper hierarchy of ability to defeat doubles teams at lower levels and win the day's event. It can be used also to sacrifice a lower level team by pitting that team against one of the opponent's top teams. All of this is done in name of winning. In some leagues this is considered a NO-NO! In others it is an acceptable part of a team's strategy. The particular leagues make the protocol here and the captains should abide by the rules. Juggling players to make the most victorious teams does smack of winning at all costs, a highly undesirable quality to bring to the sport, and especially to the women's side of the sport. Yet, if it is allowed, so be it. It may just be another element in the survival of the fittest now included in ladies league play.

POSITIONING -- The Beauty of It

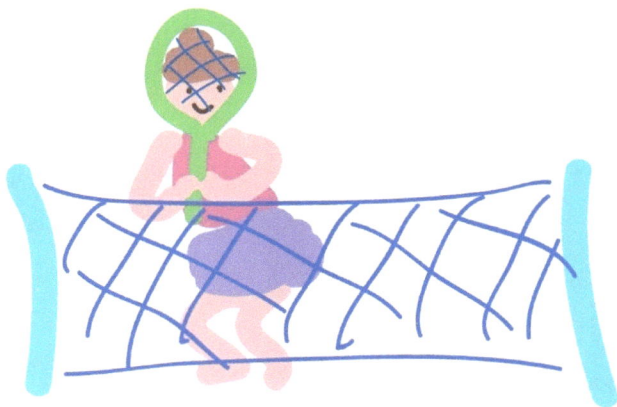

Every team normally starts with one player at net and her partner serving or receiving. This is the traditional configuration, but it changes as play begins and patterns begin to form. Chipping and charging, or serving and coming in, alter the players' locations on the court. Three may end up at net, then a lob changes that formation and another lob changes it again. This is the fun of the game -- chasing that little yellow ball wherever it goes and rebalancing your side of the net as your opponents adjust theirs.

There is really no hard and fast rule as to where to be on the court, other than the obvious ones -- that the server stand behind the baseline and the returner may not volley a return of serve. But once the ball is in play anything can happen and usually does.

There are just a couple of critical movements or court strategies that need to be mentioned, especially for the not-so-experienced players. The obvious one is that if your partner crosses to take a ball at the net or elsewhere, you must switch sides, unless one of you calls out to do otherwise.

There is another not quite so obvious move that needs to be pointed out here. If you are the target on your side of the net and the opponent has a set up, move to the alley. Do not wait to see where the ball is going to go. It is going to you! Ninety percent of the time the opponent will hit to you. You do not need to cover the center of the court. More than likely the ball will not go there.

Here's another bit of information for you if you are the target. Play close to the net. The farther back you move, the more vulnerable you become. There is more court for the opponent to hit to you. Remember, the idea is to make it difficult, or if possible to make it impossible to hit to you. Or, if they do, you are in a position to win the point. On top of the net is just such a place. By standing close to the net with your racket in front of you, anything you touch will go over the net and probably win the point. So, no one hits to someone who is standing on top of the net. If, however, you are afraid of being hit, hold the racket right in front of your face. The big racket heads that most people use now offer great protection.

In my long years of ladies league doubles play and playing with a variety of partners, there is one formation on the court that seems unknown by many. That is the down-the-line configuration.

It goes like this: your partner is engaged in the backcourt and you are at net and the play shifts from cross-court action to down-the-line shots. At this point, you must move to the centerline of the court in order to cut off any attempt by your opponent to hit behind you. The angle and opportunity will be there unless you move. This is awkward and unnatural, but necessary, whether the play is occurring on the right side of the court or the left.

As soon as the play, which always starts cross-court, moves to down-the-line, you as the net person must move toward the centerline. Do it, even if you are the weaker player. Otherwise, your opponent will eventually hit a ball behind you and win the point.

Playing the "Australian" formation when your partner is serving to the add side of the court is a good idea if your partner has a very weak backhand. By standing on the left side of the centerline and your partner serving and covering the right side of the court, your partner's backhand is protected. It can also be useful if your partner is left-handed and she is serving to the forehand court. Sometimes it's good to throw in that formation just to stir the pot and change things around. There are no set-in-concrete rules when it comes to formations.

My oftentimes partner and I have won matches in which we both stayed in the backcourt and lobbed our opponents to defeat. We have also played the "Australian" formation from the backcourt with both of us back. I stayed on my partner's left when she served to both sides, to protect her near non-existent backhand. It worked.

No structures are off limits. Figure out how you are winning points, and keep doing that. And figure out how you're losing them and change. Tennis, like life, is simple; do what works and stop doing what doesn't!

SIGNALING -- The Confusion of It

It you want to signal to your partner while you are the serving team, with the player at the net giving the signals, great. Especially great, if you know what you're doing.

Many of the teaching pros teach their league ladies how to do this and how to do it well. One of the secrets to signaling is that you have to be quick, quick on the crossover to the other side of the court, and quick to change directions if your opponent's are onto you. Sometimes the mere movement or threat of a movement jangles your opponent into missing a return. Then too, if you want to play like the pros, give signals. It's fun and it can work.

STAYING IN THE PLAY -- The Fun of It

There are just a couple of points that need to be addressed about how to remain in the play. Oftentimes league players are not aware of these and errors occur, and points are lost. For instance, if an opponent is going to hit an overhead in your direction and you are near the net, scoot backwards quickly, and then before she hits the shot, shift your weight forward. It is your only chance of staying in the play and returning the ball. Leaning backwards, you will have no chance.

Here is something else to consider. You may have noticed how some players always get to the ball while others never quite make it. These players appear to have their feet on a delay timer. It's not that their feet are stuck in cement; it is that they wait until a ball is hit and know exactly where it's going before they react. How to know where a ball is going before it is hit is a useful thing to know. Just take a look at the face of the hitter's racket. Is it angled in a certain direction or is it facing forward? Then, get going in that direction. Simple observations are a big help to being at the right place at the right time, and not a second too late.

This brings up another important point that many Club Players overlook -- the importance of movement. STAY IN MOTION! Keep moving. Many league players are not in the habit of being in motion continuously. They start and stop. Oftentimes the pattern is: hit, stand, walk, hit, stand, etc. If you've got toes, get on them. Bounce, dance, stay fluid. You'll have a better chance of staying in the play if you stay in motion. And, if you guess wrong, it is easier to change directions than it is to start from a dead standstill. Like any good scout: Be Prepared! Preparing is moving, even if it is only slightly. In this way you're always "ready."

There are very few places an adult can romp around, and move freely like a child, but a tennis court is one of them. Let your hair down; kick up your heels and dance. The ball flying back and forth across the net sets up a lovely rhythm, sometimes a waltz, sometimes a fox trot, or even a Charleston. Put on those high-heel sneakers and boogie!

Once you're into the dance of the game, you will not be tempted to do that foolish-of-all-things -- chide or beret yourself for missing a shot. No one gets upset with themselves or their partner on the dance floor if a step is missed or a trip occurs, nor should you on the tennis court.

I've seen players, mostly women, come to a complete stop in their play to scold themselves even before the point is over. Play must be continuous. That means everyone. No stopping for criticism or self-coaching. Keep going; you never know when your opponent will miss an overhead.

Let your whole body play. Many beginners and also many regular Club Players play only with their arms. They run. They stop. They swing the racket with one arm, and nothing else gets to participate. Try using your whole body when you swing at the ball. The more you use, the more powerful the shot.

Tennis is about playing, not winning. You may win, but you'll play better if you just play.

FOCUSING -- The Love of It

The lack of focus is one of the leading causes of shot fatality in tennis. Focus! Focus! Focus! How do you do it without continually hammering yourself to do it? Through love! Love is the great binder in life. If you love the ball, love hitting the ball, and look forward to its arrival on your side of the net, your focus is perfect; it is on the ball. If you fear that you might miss a ball when it comes toward you, your focus is split; it's now on you and the ball. The idea is to get all of your energies lined up and going in one direction --

toward the on-coming ball -- by welcoming it, and then redirecting it where you would like it to go.

Here is another spin on your attitude toward a ball that is coming your way. That old expression: "As you think, so it will be," is particularly true in regards to a ball you're about to hit. If you think a ball is difficult, it will be. If you think it is easy, it will certainly be easier to handle than if you think otherwise. A particular shot may require more effort on your part. However, see how clever your body is in adjusting to a shot if you relax into it and not typecast it as "difficult." It can be challenging, which is fun, but never let it be "difficult." Get comfortable with being uncomfortable. Get comfortable with not being in the perfect position. No one wants to hit you something you like; better if you learn to like whatever they hit.

Keep in mind that the ball always wins, so stay attached to it; make it your best friend -- be one with the ball. Leave the hopes and demands of your teammates on the sideline, along with your own. Play stress-free. Play happy.

THE PRIZE

There is no greater prize in tennis than the opportunity to play. And, there is no greater game than tennis. Everyone can afford a racket, a pair of sneakers, a can of balls, and can drop in at any public park courts and find someone to hit with.

If you've got a son, a daughter, a grandson or granddaughter, teach that child how to play this marvelous game well enough to play on a high school team and that child will have friends for life, no matter where he or she may go. Wonderful people are involved in this sport and the sport itself opens doors, through the people one meets, to life-long friendships, business connections, and even love.

There is no end to the benefits this game offers. An hour of running around a tennis court is the best cardio-vascular exercise you can find -- no gym fee, no stale air, plus lots of sunshine. It suits the graceful, those who prefer to approach the movements as dance. It offers muscular development for the young. It is vigorous enough for the macho types, and gentle enough for the senior citizens. It can be a meditation, a tai chi exercise, a workout, or a waltz. But whatever it is for you, it is good.

And when you take this wonderful game of tennis, put a pink ribbon around it, you have ladies league tennis -- a delightful morning of fun, food, fashion, friendship, and play.

ENJOY!

(Many thanks to the leaders of ALTA, the league supervisors at the USTA, and the many league coordinators and captains around the country who have spent endless hours on the phone, sending e-mails or texts to organize each week's play.)

Here is another wonderful tennis book by Sally Huss.

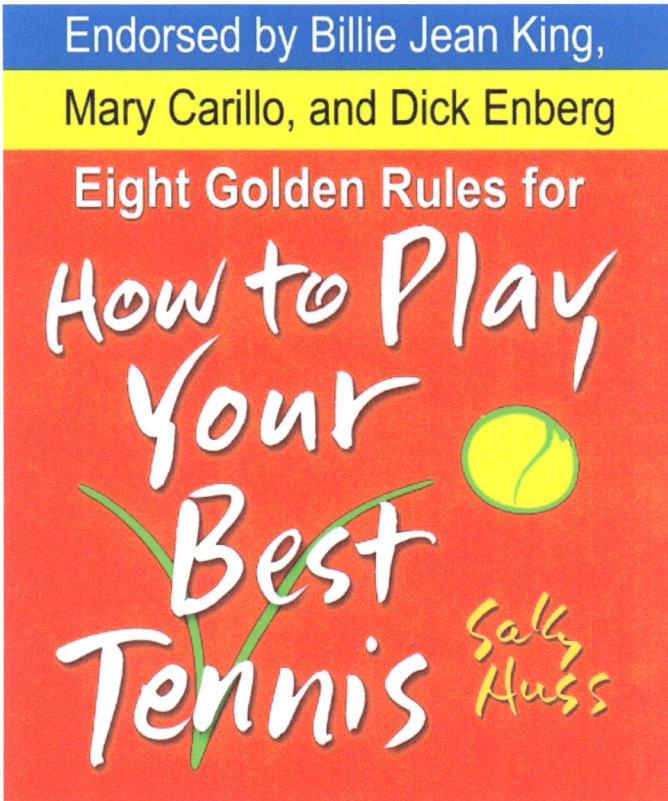

Endorsed by Billie Jean King, Mary Carillo, and Dick Enberg

Eight Golden Rules for How to Play Your Best Tennis

Sally Huss

Mary Carillo, CBS and ESPN Sports:

"Sally Huss has written a simple, sparkling gem of a book. It is wise and gentle, and gives to tennis players what the great UCLA coach John Wooden gave to basketball players with his Pyramid of Success. If you do what Sally suggests you will be more than a better player; you'll be a better person. Perhaps her book should be called *Eight Golden Rules for How To Live Your Best Life.*"

Dick Enberg, CBS and ESPN Sports:

"Loved the book. I've seen Sally Huss play this great game of tennis. She caressed the ball, while fully embracing the experience. Her style and good form are expressed in her *EIGHT GOLDEN RULES FOR HOW TO PLAY YOUR BEST TENNIS.* It's an extension of her proven championship play. The message in her book is direct, kind, respectful, and in its wondrous simplicity, as sharp as a backhand winner down the line. If I were to start playing again, I'd be best served to read this book FIRST and then GRIP a racquet. Game, Set, and Match, Ms. Huss! Oh My!"

Billie Jean King, 39 Grand Slam Titles, Founder of World Team Tennis:

"Tennis is a lifetime sport and fun for players of all ages. In *Eight Golden Rules for How to Play Your Best Tennis*, Sally Huss shows you how to get the most out of your game and how much fun playing tennis can be."

EIGHT GOLDEN RULES FOR HOW TO PLAY YOUR BEST TENNIS may be found on Amazon as an e-book or soft cover book -- http://amzn.com/B004QOAGL4.

If you liked LOVE LADIES LEAGUE TENNIS, please be kind enough to post a short review on Amazon by using this link: http://amzn.com/B00I2XPUF2.

You may wish to join our Family of Friends to receive information about upcoming FREE e-book promotions and download a free poster – "Happiness on an Elephant" on Sally's website -- http://www.sallyhuss.com. Thank You.

More Sally Huss books may be viewed on the Author's Profile on Amazon. Here is that URL: http://amzn.to/VpR7B8.

About the Author/Illustrator

Sally Huss

Sally Huss was a National and Wimbledon Junior Champion, a Wimbledon semi-finalist in singles and doubles, winner of many National senior singles and doubles titles, and still plays ladies league tennis!

"Bright and happy," "light and whimsical" have been the catch phrases attached to the writings and art of Sally Huss for over 30 years. From inspirational books, children's books to her King Features syndicated newspaper panel "Happy Musings," all of her creations are happy in nature and free-spirited in style.

Sally is a graduate of USC with a degree in Fine Art and through the years has had 26 of her own licensed art galleries throughout the world.

LOVE LADIES LEAGUE TENNIS
By Sally Huss

Copyright 2014 Sally Huss
Huss Publishing

No part of this publication may be reproduced, sold, stored in a retrieval system, or transmitted in any form, or by any means (electronic, mechanical, photocopying, resending or otherwise) without permission by the author.

Love Ladies League Tennis

www.ingramcontent.com/pod-product-compliance
Lightning Source LLC
Chambersburg PA
CBHW041802040426
42448CB00001B/18

* 9 7 8 0 6 9 2 3 6 6 6 6 0 *